THE FORCES

Sue Graves

Rising Stars UK Ltd.
22 Grafton Street, London W1S 4EX
www.risingstars-uk.com

nasen
Helping Everyone Achieve

NASEN House, 4/5 Amber Business Village, Amber Close, Amington, Tamworth,
Staffordshire B77 4RP

All facts are correct at time of going to press.

Published 2008
Text, design and layout © Rising Stars UK Ltd.

Series Consultant: Lorraine Petersen
Cover design: Neil Straker Creative
Design: Clive Sutherland
Editorial: Frances Ridley
Illustrations: Bill Greenhead for Illustrations Ltd
Photographs:
Alamy: 19, 22, 26-27, 36, 38, 40, 45
Corbis: 20, 28-29, 33, 34-35, 42
Getty Images: 4, 8, 30
iStockphoto.com: 10-11
PA Photos: 18

© Crown Copyright/MOD, image from www.photos.mod.uk. Reproduced with the
permission of the Controller of Her Majesty's Stationery Office
p12: Photograph by: Darren Casey; p13: Photograph by: LA (PHOT) Stubbens;
p14: LA (PHOT) Ray Jones; p23: Jon Ryder; p23: Stuart Bingham;
p41: POA (PHOT) Sean Clee

British Library Cataloguing in Publication Data.
A CIP record for this book is available from the British Library.

ISBN: 978-1-84680-451-9

Printed by: Craftprint International Ltd, Singapore

Contents

THE FORCES: THE BIG PICTURE

The forces are the army, the navy and the air force.
They protect the UK from attack by other countries.
Many other countries have forces like these.

FOCUS

Find the answers to these questions.

1 Who carries small **harpoons**?
2 What is a military **tattoo**?
3 How close to the ground is a low-flying helicopter?

 # ZOOMING IN ...

Ready for action

Flying high

Forces keep the peace

All hands on deck

The end of a
mission

Training to fight

Forces from
around the world

THE NAVY

A navy is made up of ships, submarines and other craft. It also includes the men and women who serve on these craft. Many countries that border the sea have a navy. It protects the country from attack by sea.

SCENE: A Royal Navy recruitment centre.

CAST:
Officer Harris: a Royal Navy recruitment officer.
Becky Davis: a woman aged 25 – she wants to join the navy.

OFFICER HARRIS: How did you find out about the Royal Navy?

BECKY DAVIS: I went on the Royal Navy website. I also sent off for some information about it.

OFFICER HARRIS: Why do you want to join?

BECKY DAVIS: I want to do more with my life.

OFFICER HARRIS: What do you mean?

BECKY DAVIS:	Well, I left school at 16. I went to work in an office. My job is boring and I have no **prospects**. I want to learn different skills. Also, I would like to serve my country.
OFFICER HARRIS:	What skills can you offer the navy?
BECKY DAVIS:	I work hard and I have good people skills. I have good computer skills, too.
OFFICER HARRIS:	And what skills would you like to learn?
BECKY DAVIS:	I've always enjoyed cooking. My goal is to work as a Royal Navy cook.

Joining up

To join the Royal Navy you must be:

- 16 years old
- fit and healthy
- ready to go to anywhere in the world.

Some jobs have special rules. You must be:

- at least 166 cm tall to be an **aircraft handler**
- a British citizen to join the submarine service
- a man to join the Royal Marine Commandos.

A new recruit

Royal Marine Commando

FORCES FACT

- Benin is a small country in Africa – it only has 5 ships and 100 people in its navy.
- The US Navy has over 500,000 people – it's the largest navy in the world!

LIFE AT SEA

RN recruits are sent on training missions at sea. The recruits in this picture are on board an **aircraft carrier**. They have been training for war. They learned how to look after the ship and how to fly planes off and on to the ship safely.

Diary of a Royal Navy Recruit

Friday: I'm so glad I trained as a **medical assistant.** Today has been brilliant. I trained ten people in first aid. I showed them how to give first aid if somebody collapses. I showed them how to put a patient in the recovery position. Then I showed them how to bandage a wound.

Later on, I had to work in the sick bay. We have three patients in there at the moment. Luckily, nobody is in for anything serious.

At 1600 hours, I helped to clean the ship. I cleaned the decks and did some polishing, too. We work as a team on board ship. Everybody helps to keep the ship clean and tidy. It's hard work but it keeps you fit!

On board an aircraft carrier

A mission on an aircraft carrier can last for weeks or months. Life on board is always busy. People do different jobs. Some fly the aircraft. Others look after the aircraft and ship. There are medical staff and catering staff.

Directing an aircraft on to the ship.

Working out in the gym.

The ship also has living quarters. This is where people eat, sleep and relax after work. Some people go to the gym. Other people send letters, cards and emails to their family and friends.

THE ARMY

An army is a large group of soldiers. The soldiers are trained to fight wars on land. Many countries have an army. An army protects its country from attack. It also helps its country when natural disasters strike — like floods and earthquakes.

WHAT DO YOU WANT OUT OF LIFE?

Do you want adventure?

Do you enjoy a challenge?

Then an army career might be right for you.

What skills do you want to learn?

What job do you want to do?

The army offers a wide choice of jobs and training.

There are lots of good reasons to join the army!

Play your favourite sports – and learn new ones.

See the world – and help to make it a safer place.

You can make a difference!

Join the army ... and see how far you can go!

The SAS

The **SAS** is a special team in the British Army. It does dangerous jobs around the world. It rescues **hostages** and captures **terrorists**. The SAS never identify their soldiers to the public. This protects SAS soldiers and their families from revenge attacks.

SAS soldiers wear special clothes and carry special equipment on their missions.

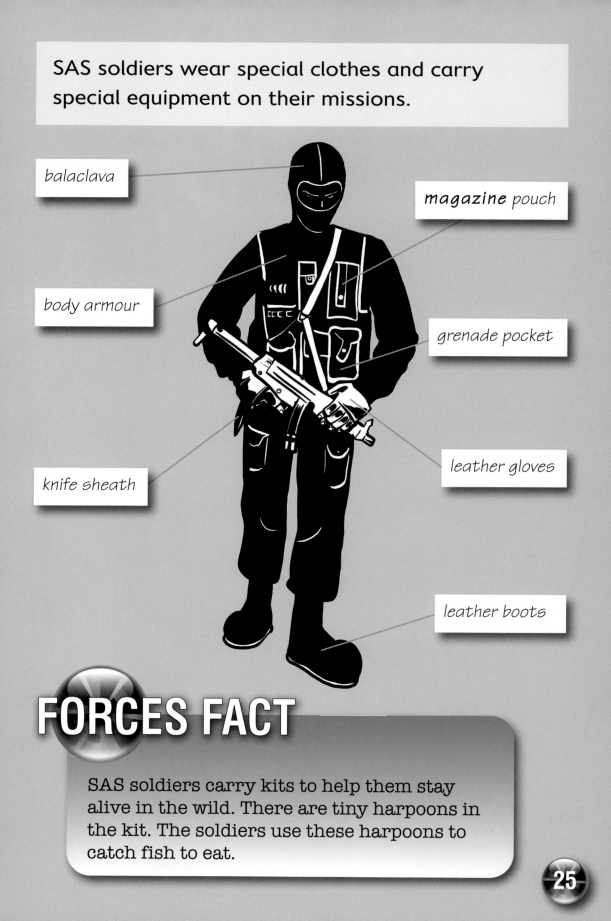

balaclava

magazine pouch

body armour

grenade pocket

knife sheath

leather gloves

leather boots

FORCES FACT

SAS soldiers carry kits to help them stay alive in the wild. There are tiny harpoons in the kit. The soldiers use these harpoons to catch fish to eat.

CLOSE-UP:
THE MILITARY TATTOO

Every year there is a military tattoo in Edinburgh in Scotland. Forces come from all over the world to take part. They come to show off their skills to the public.

At a tattoo, forces from around the world perform special **drills**. The gun drill is very exciting to watch. The forces take the gun apart so that it can be moved. Then they put it back together again.

KEEPING THE PEACE

Armies don't just fight wars - they help to keep
the peace, too. The **UN** sends peace-keeping
forces to countries where there has been fighting.
These forces are called 'The Blue Helmets'.
They wear blue helmets so that they are easy
to identify.

Peacekeeping report 29th July 06

Report by:

Major Jim Dent, UN Peacekeeping Corps.

Situation:

Elections for a new president and National Assembly in the Congo in Africa.

Status:

Peaceful but there have been reports that some people are scared to vote. They think they will be attacked by the rebels.

Action:

• We have placed soldiers at all voting stations. We want to make sure that people can vote freely and safely.

• Some people have come early to the voting stations. They have to wait in the heat for hours at a time. Our soldiers are giving them water to drink and first aid where it is needed.

The UN spent $1 billion on the peace-keeping mission in the Congo.

Send in the army!

Soldiers are trained to fight wars and to keep the peace. They are also trained to help in emergencies. They do this in their own countries and in countries around the world.

Soldiers are trained to:
- look for people trapped in earthquakes
- search for people lost in the jungle
- search for people lost in the desert
- rescue people trapped in floods
- get food to people in a **famine**.

HIGH FLYERS

Most countries have an air force. An air force protects its country from air attacks. The British Air Force is called the **RAF**. People in the RAF are trained to do many different jobs. RAF pilots are very highly trained.

Welcome to RAF Valley

RAF Valley is an RAF Station. It's on the island of Anglesey in North Wales. Its main job is to give advance pilot training. This training prepares RAF pilots for war. The pilots fly BAE Hawks for this important training.

A BAE Hawk

Explore this website to find out more about RAF Valley.

History of RAF Valley

Events

A Sea King Helicopter rescues people from Mount Snowdon – the highest mountain in Wales.

RAF Valley is also home to the Sea King Helicopters and their crews. These helicopters take part in search and rescue operations. They rescue people stranded on ships in the Irish Sea. Helicopter crews also take part in mountain rescue work.

News   Meet the pilots

Flying low

All RAF pilots learn to fly low. It's an important skill in war and in peace.

Fast jet **combat** pilots are trained to fly fast and low. This is so they can fly beneath enemy **radar**!

Helicopter pilots are trained to fly low. This is so they can:

- drop troops quickly during fighting
- get to places that are difficult to reach
- search for people
- rescue people.

FORCES FACT

A helicopter pilot is flying low if he is 500 feet above the ground or lower!

TRAINING

People in the RAF have to be ready to go to war.
They must be ready for action at all times.
They're sent on special drills to perfect their skills.
These drills are called manoeuvres.

RAF Cornwall

5th September

Dear Mum and Dad,

Hope you are both OK. I'm in Cornwall on manoeuvres. We got here last Monday and will stay for three weeks.

The manoeuvres are going well but we've got a lot to practise. On some manoeuvres we're training to move troops quickly. On others, we're training to move heavy equipment from one place to another. Yesterday, two of the heavy trucks got bogged down in mud. Nightmare!

I have to check that the planes are always ready to fly. I have to look after the engines and check that they work. We've set up a small **mobile** workshop to deal with engine problems. It's hard work – but great!

I'll try to write again soon.

From

Danny

RAF engineers

One in three people in the RAF is an **engineer**. Engineers look after all the moving parts of the planes. They check the planes before the pilots fly them. They make sure the plane is safe to fly.

Wings – checked for faults such as cracks. Wings may need to be repaired.

Engines – checked to make sure parts are working well. Parts may need to be repaired or replaced.

Tyres – checked for cuts or splits. Cut or split tyres are changed.

GLOSSARY

Aircraft carrier	a ship that carries planes – planes can fly off the ship and land on it.
Aircraft handler	person who checks that planes can land and take off safely
Combat	fighting during a war
Drill(s)	doing something over and over again to get it right
Engineer	person who makes engines or looks after them
Famine	when there is not enough food to feed people
Harpoon(s)	a special spear for catching fish
Hostage(s)	a person taken prisoner by somebody who might hurt or kill them if they don't get want they want
Magazine	holds bullets – the bullets are fed automatically into a gun.
Medical assistant	a member of a medical team
Mission	a special task
Mobile	can be moved around
Prospects	chances of success in a job or a career
Radar	a system that uses radio signals to find the exact position of an aircraft or a ship
RAF	stands for Royal Air Force – the RAF is the British air force
SAS	stands for Special Air Service
Tattoo	music and marching show
Terrorist(s)	person who uses violence against a government
UN	stands for United Nations

INDEX